EXPLORING HI-TECH JOBS

Hi-Tech Jobs in SCIENCE

Terri Dougherty

San Diego, CA

© 2024 ReferencePoint Press, Inc.
Printed in the United States

For more information, contact:
ReferencePoint Press, Inc.
PO Box 27779
San Diego, CA 92198
www.ReferencePointPress.com

ALL RIGHTS RESERVED.
No part of this work covered by the copyright hereon may be reproduced or used in any form or by any means—graphic, electronic, or mechanical, including photocopying, recording, taping, web distribution, or information storage retrieval systems—without the written permission of the publisher.

LIBRARY OF CONGRESS CATALOGING-IN-PUBLICATION DATA

Names: Dougherty, Terri- author.
Title: Hi-tech jobs in science / by Terri Dougherty.
Description: San Diego, CA : ReferencePoint Press, Inc., 2024. | Series: Exploring hi-tech jobs | Includes bibliographical references and index.
Identifiers: LCCN 2023041472 (print) | ISBN 9781678207083 (library binding) | ISBN 9781678207090 (ebook)
Subjects: LCSH: Science--Vocational guidance--Juvenile literature.

Contents

Introduction: Jobs That Can Change the World	**4**
AI Computer and Information Research Scientist	**6**
Environmental Scientist	**13**
Biomedical Engineer	**21**
Materials Scientist	**29**
Data Scientist	**37**
Food Scientist	**45**
Source Notes	53
Interview with a Food Scientist	57
Other Jobs in Science	60
Index	61
Picture Credits	64
About the Author	64

Introduction: Jobs That Can Change the World

When she thought about what she wanted to do with her life, Erin Lavik was sure of one thing: she wanted to make a difference. That is why she decided to turn her focus to biomedical engineering. As a result, she has designed implants that could one day treat spinal cord injuries. She also has overseen a team of students researching ways to stop internal bleeding.

People like Lavik who work in high-tech science careers have the opportunity to change the world. They seek to improve the way things are done, and they use cutting-edge technology to do it. Those working in these careers get to be creative, design new things, help people live better lives, and solve problems.

High-tech science careers offer a variety of job choices, a good salary, and job security. There is high demand for people with a background in science and technology, and the job outlook is strong. Employment in science, technology, engineering, and mathematics (STEM) occupations is expected to increase by 1,064,000 jobs and grow by 10.8 percent by 2031, according to the Bureau of Labor Statistics. The average annual salary is $95,420, much higher than the average salary for non-STEM occupations of $40,120.

Being inquisitive and wondering how things work are great traits for people who are interested in high-tech science careers. "I've always been curious about the world around me,"[1] Lavik says. This curiosity can lead to new discoveries and breakthroughs. Scientists at Ames National Laboratory, a US Department of Energy National Laboratory, solved an eighty-year-old mystery because they became curious about a molecule's structure. Scientists at this laboratory, operated by Iowa State University, focus on creating materials and energy solutions. While conducting research, they found a description from the 1940s of the same reaction they were working on. They used advanced technology to uncover the structure of the boron monoxide molecule, which had eluded researchers decades earlier. "What really excites me is just the fact that this is an old problem," says Frederic Perras, a research team member. "It's such a basic material. . . . So, it's interesting from that point of view that we finally solved its structure."[2] Now that the mystery has been solved, it could lead to the creation of innovative, useful materials.

Those working in high-tech science careers sometimes find themselves venturing into the unknown. They may be faced with new computer systems or other unfamiliar equipment, but this should not be a barrier. "Don't be afraid of technology," says Marilyn Jackson, chief executive officer (CEO) of UnderGrid Networks and a digital strategist who works with artificial intelligence (AI). "You may not understand what that is. Do not let that hinder you. Having the intestinal fortitude to jump in, even to those things that you don't understand is going to be very, very key because those are the opportunities that create great output."[3]

People who work in high-tech jobs need to enjoy the process of learning new things because technology is constantly evolving. Technology that was considered high-tech twenty years ago is considered standard today. Jackson's continued interest in staying on top of the latest technology has helped her advance in her career. After high school, she got a computer engineering degree from the University of Texas. She did not stop there, however. During her career she has consistently received additional training on new systems. "In this career field . . . you're a lifelong learner because the industry never stops training," she explains. "If there's a technical class or if there's a class for improvement or a class on a new language, I'm there."[4]

The result of her dedication to learning is self-confidence and a rewarding career. "My confidence comes from knowing what I know," she asserts. "I'm very solid in what I've learned along my journey and that gives me the confidence to do a lot of the things that I do."[5]

AI Computer and Information Research Scientist

What Does an AI Computer and Information Research Scientist Do?

Josh Tobin makes AI systems more accurate. AI computer systems use data to make predictions, and machine learning allows them to become more precise on the basis of the patterns that are found. Tobin and his team help companies retrain computer systems so they do a better job of continuously learning. "The main challenge in building or adapting infrastructure for machine learning is that the field moves incredibly quickly,"[6] says Tobin.

Researcher Jun Kato focuses on using AI to support creativity. He and his colleagues are working on apps that merge lyrics, music, and video. This allows those creating the videos to focus on visual style rather than worrying about synchronizing graphics with beats and vocals. "Nowadays, all kinds of artistic activities use the computer as a tool,"[7] he comments.

Alexander Kotev, an associate professor of computer science at Wayne State University, is looking at how AI can help people lose

A Few Facts

Number of Jobs
33,500

Pay
$131,490 per year

Educational Requirements
Master's degree in computer science or a related field

Personal Qualities
Curiosity, problem-solving, communication, analytical skills, logical thinking, detail oriented

Work Settings
Office

Future Job Outlook
Projected to grow by 21 percent through 2031

weight. He is working with health experts to develop an AI program that uses counseling to motivate people to make diet and lifestyle changes. "We are hopeful that modern AI technologies can have a positive impact on people's physical and mental health,"[8] he says.

AI computer and information research scientists find ways to make massive amounts of data useful. They help people work more efficiently by designing computer programs that pull relevant information together and present it in a usable way. Their programs might analyze data from an experiment's results, test a software system, answer questions, or predict weather patterns. To do this, AI computer and information research scientists design computer languages and software systems. They make and improve algorithms, which are the instructions that tell a computer what to do. Their programs allow computers to quickly and efficiently perform a task, solve a problem, or deliver meaningful content or data.

Work done by AI computer and information research scientists propels advances in medicine, science, and business and helps people in their daily lives. Researcher Cynthia Breazeal works with human-robot interaction at the Massachusetts Institute of Technology. Her group investigates how robots can be used in education, health, aging, and wellness. She has developed robots such as Cog, which can track faces and grab objects, and Jibo, a robot that can provide companionship. "It's about finding ways to use robots to support people,"[9] she explains.

A Typical Workday

AI researcher Rik Koncel-Kedziorski spends much of his day learning about advances in AI and working to improve AI systems. His goal is to get computer networks to do a better job of answering questions. "I spend 85 percent of my time learning and 15 percent innovating,"[10] says Koncel-Kedziorski, who works for an AI solutions firm. His work also involves reflecting—digesting what he has learned to come up with new insights.

Innovation Strikes on Its Own Time

"A lot of the actual learning and innovating takes place absent any direct action toward those goals. The brain seems to do some kind of 'brain magic' in its own time, on its own schedule. . . . I will be washing dishes or sailing the boat on a weekend, and meanwhile my brain is busy synthesizing what was learned and innovated in the last week all on its own. Regularly, I will be struck with a powerful new insight or direction for future research while in the middle of some non-work activity and must quickly jot it down in my Notes app for future consideration."

—Rik Koncel-Kedziorski, AI researcher

Rik Koncel-Kedziorski, "A Day in the Life of an AI Researcher," *Kensho Blog*, May 16, 2023. https://blog.kensho.com.

The learning part of Koncel-Kedziorski's day involves activities that help to bring about a deeper understanding of the field and exposure to new ideas. Most days he reads other people's research papers and talks to researchers working in other areas. "I need to be well aware of what peers and industry colleagues have been doing before I can do anything they haven't already done," he explains. Each week, he also dives into a math concept that challenges him. "Studying almost any math seems to make me smarter in complex and diffuse ways,"[11] he says. The concept might be different than the math he uses in a typical day, and he might not even completely understand it, but looking at it closely helps him sharpen his skills.

When innovating, Koncel-Kedziorski writes code and collaborates with others. He looks for insights into how AI works and aims to get it to deliver better results. "It can be a slow and painful process," he admits. "If I do my job well, I can invent something exciting and useful not only to the AI research community but to the world at large."[12]

For AI researcher Nicolai Nielsen, much of the day is spent in coding sessions lasting two to four hours. "I just try to be as focused as possible when I'm at work because then I can relax and recharge my batteries when I'm doing something else besides work," he says. He takes a midmorning break to walk his dog and spends some time researching new topics. "Usually I place this session in the middle of the day because then I can get a break," he says. "I just recharge and I can do another coding session after that." After his second coding session of the day, he often heads to the gym. "When I go to the gym I gain so much new energy I can actually do more work when I get home,"[13] he comments.

Education and Training

A person working in AI computer and information research science often has a master's degree in computer science or a related field, such as computer engineering. Earning a master's degree usually involves going to school for an additional two to three years after obtaining a bachelor's degree. A job in this field may also require a doctorate, which requires additional schooling. Jan Leike, who leads the alignment team at AI research and development firm OpenAI, suggests that those interested in an AI career earn an undergraduate degree in computer science and mathematics and aim to eventually earn a doctorate.

Even after they have their degree, AI computer and information research scientists do not stop learning. For example, researchers at the banking and financial services firm JPMorgan, who work to develop machine learning models for workflows and trading platforms, attend conferences to learn about new developments and bring ideas into the organization. "We come back from a conference knowing where the field is and how to take those state of the art methods and apply them to problems in the bank,"[14] comments Lidia Mangu, the head of the Machine Learning Center of Excellence at the company.

Skills and Personality

AI computer and information research scientists should be good at solving problems and thinking critically. They also must be innovative and creative when it comes to solving problems, so

Looking for People Who Are Always Experimenting

"In a way, we don't actually make a strong distinction between research engineer and research scientist at OpenAI. In each of these roles, you're expected to write code, and you're expected to run your own experiments. And in fact, I think it's really important to always be running lots of experiments, small experiments, testing your ideas quickly, and then iterating and trying to learn more about the world."

—Jan Leike, alignment team leader at OpenAI

Quoted in Robert Wiblin and Keiran Harris, "Jan Leike on OpenAI's Massive Push to Make Superintelligence Safe in 4 Years or Less," 80,000 Hours (podcast), August 7, 2023. https://80000hours.org

they can find new ways to apply technology. Marilyn Jackson of UnderGrid Networks has always been curious. "I've always tinkered," she recalls. "There were instances where my brother and I would destroy appliances and I was good at taking them apart but he was better at putting them back together. But certainly the curiosity made me take them apart."[15]

Having the persistence to solve puzzles and problems is also beneficial. "You should be comfortable with navigating a space that you don't really understand very well, because researchers kind of necessarily are on the frontier of human knowledge and things that we understand, so you have to be comfortable with the unknown,"[16] Leike says.

When looking for scientists and others to work on a team looking to improve AI and make it safer to use, Leike noted that technical skills are important because ideas will need to be tested. Although scientists need to understand how language models that generate human-like answers work—and how to make them work better—curiosity is also necessary. "In general, you need a lot of critical thinking, and asking important questions, and being very curious about the world and the technology that we're building,"[17] he advised.

AI researchers often collaborate with others and should have good listening, speaking, and writing skills. Papers need to be prepared for publication in academic journals, and research is presented at conferences. Research results need to be explained in simple terms that can be understood by someone without a technical background.

Working Conditions
AI computer and information research scientists typically work indoors at a computer in an office setting. Some work from home and/or alternate between home and office.

Employers and Earnings
AI computer and information research scientists often work for companies that design computer system software or for the federal government. They may also work in a business's information technology area to develop AI programs that make the best use of a company's data. In addition, they work at universities, where they conduct research and collaborate with businesses to create AI programs.

The median pay for computer and information research scientists (which means that half earned more, and half earned less) was $131,490 in 2021. The top 10 percent earned $208,000, and the bottom 10 percent earned $74,210. The highest-paying field was computer systems design and related services, which paid a median annual wage of $161,860. Software publishers had the next-highest salary, at $152,490.

Future Outlook
The job outlook for computer and information research scientists is very bright. The Bureau of Labor Statistics reports that openings are projected to grow by 21 percent through 2031, which is much faster

than average. More than thirty-three hundred openings are expected for computer and information research scientists each year.

AI computer and information research scientists will be needed to help companies use the new technology to their benefit. As AI becomes more prominent, these companies will also need to ensure that AI systems do not cause problems, are safe to use, and work as intended.

Find Out More

Career Girls
www.careergirls.org
This website helps girls explore careers in information technology, STEM, business, and other areas. Its videos feature diverse role models in a variety of occupations. The college prep section provides advice and information on college majors.

Frontiers in Artificial Intelligence
www.frontiersin.org/journals/artificial-intelligence
This website brings together articles on AI innovation across a broad array of areas. As a result, it offers a look at how AI can be applied in numerous ways. Business, finance, energy, and medicine are addressed, as well as natural language processing and machine learning.

IEEE Computer Society
www.computer.org/about
Numerous articles about the latest advances in AI and other computer-related topics are found in the "Publications" section of this Institute of Electrical and Electronics Engineers (IEEE) website. The site also includes information on tech news and trends as well as information about education for software engineers. Online courses are offered.

Environmental Scientist

What Does an Environmental Scientist Do?

Madison Trowbridge's workday might involve analyzing data on a computer or heading out on a boat to gather water samples from the rivers and bays of southwest Florida that are fed by springs. "No matter the long days or the sunburns, working on the springs never gets old," she says. "Every field day takes my breath away just like the first time I visited the springs and I still get excited every time I see an otter or a manatee."[18]

Lesley-Ann Dupigny-Giroux also spends time making observations outdoors. As a climatologist, she works in an area of environmental science that focuses on studying the long-term impact of weather patterns on an area. She gathers and analyzes data and shares her findings and knowledge. "Doing a lot of computer-based work and being out and making observations, or connecting with people one-on-one, giving presentations, they're all part of the same thing which is sharing my knowledge and understanding,"[19] she comments.

Wu Sun is researching better ways to determine how changes

A Few Facts

Number of Jobs
80,000

Pay
$76,530 per year

Educational Requirements
Bachelor's degree in natural science or environmental science

Personal Qualities
Analytical, communication, problem-solving, interpersonal skills, self-discipline

Work Settings
Laboratory; in the field

Future Job Outlook
Projected to grow by 5 percent through 2031

in temperature impact the amount of carbon that plants can pull from the atmosphere. He works with other researchers to take measurements from dozens of monitoring stations in North America. "This is absolutely crucial for refining our climate change projections and for informing migration strategies,"[20] Sun explains.

Environmental scientists study the natural world and look for solutions to environmental problems. They use computer programs to analyze information and also gather data using air, soil, and water samples. Using knowledge of biology, chemistry, and geology, they evaluate their findings. They might uncover information about soil pollution or chemicals in the water that pose health risks. They could work to restore polluted land and make water safe to drink. Protecting the environment and human health are both part of the job of an environmental scientist.

The discoveries uncovered by environmental scientists are used by businesses and government agencies. Environmental scientists work with companies to help make sure construction projects impact the environment as little as possible. They also monitor the water at local beaches to ensure conditions are safe for swimming. Some environmental scientists work to develop regulations that help protect wetlands and support clean air, soil, and water; others work for companies that help businesses understand how to comply with these regulations.

An environmental scientist can specialize in a number of areas. A climatologist or a climate change analyst looks at how weather trends and changes affect different regions and environments. An industrial ecologist helps companies understand how their manufacturing processes affect the environment. A polluted piece of land could be cleaned up effectively thanks to assessments done by an environmental restoration planner. Likewise, environmental chemists use their understanding of how chemicals react in various ecosystems to help clean up contaminated soil, water, and air.

Helping Others

"If there's somebody that could be helped by something that I've observed or some piece of the puzzle that I've been able [to] contribute to, that's essentially what drives me and what makes me tick."

—Lesley-Ann Dupigny-Giroux, climatologist

Quoted in Lake Champlain Basin Program, "Meet the Scientist: Observations and Patterns with Lesley-Ann Dupigny-Giroux, PhD," YouTube, April 11, 2023. https://www.youtube.com/watch?v=3SHoomcR_3E.

The Workday

Environmental scientist Amanda Montgomery has a desk in an office, but she also spends time outdoors. She gathers information about an area's environmental characteristics for organizations looking to build roads, buildings, or other structures. These companies need to comply with environmental regulations, and Montgomery helps them do that. For one roadway project, she classified soils, surveyed trees, and looked for other indicators to determine the limits of a wetland. "We'll give all that information to our roadway designers and they . . . incorporate it into their roadway designs,"[21] she explains.

Trowbridge also splits her time between outdoor work in the field and time in the office. Every workday is different. "I can be out in the field one day and sitting at my desk reading about research from halfway across the world the next," she says. "Even in a single day, a scientist can switch tasks from analyzing data, to writing technical reports, to reading research articles."[22]

Dupigny-Giroux also divides her time between field observations, data analysis, and presentations. To gather data, she uses high-tech equipment. "I use remote sensing imagery in most of my work because the data that we acquire from airplanes, drones, and satellites allow us to see patterns that would not be

The work of environmental scientists involves protecting the environment and human health. Those who study water quality might take samples that will be tested for signs of pollutants that could harm humans and wildlife.

readily observable from the ground," she says. "These images can be combined into color composites or analyzed by software, which helps us to visualize and quantify details that aren't visible to the naked eye."[23] As a professor at the University of Vermont, Dupigny-Giroux also shares her findings, which she considers to be an important part of her work. "I give presentations to pretty much everybody who asks," she comments. "As an educator, that is one of my biggest contributions, to be able to share that latest cutting edge study that helps to move the needle in our understanding."[24]

Education and Training

A bachelor's degree in environmental science or another field related to natural resources is usually needed to become an environmental scientist, although a student who wants to pursue a master's or doctorate degree may study a specific area, such as geology, chemistry, or physics. An individual interested in specializing in climatology may work toward a degree in climatology, meteorology, or atmospheric science. Montgomery became an environmental scientist after earning a bachelor's degree in biological sciences and a master's degree in marine biology.

Classes often include biology, chemistry, physics, and geology. Students may also take courses in waste management and environmental laws. After graduating from college, environmental scientists may earn a certificate in areas such as hazardous materials management or environmental management to show their expertise.

A professor like Dupigny-Giroux has additional schooling beyond a bachelor's degree. In addition to a bachelor's degree in physical geography and development studies, she has a master's degree in climatology and hydrology and a doctorate in climatology and geographic information systems.

While in school, students often have an internship that allows them to apply what they have learned in the classroom. During their internship, they may work with computer modeling and data analysis programs as well as geographic information systems.

Skills and Personality

An interest in the environment and geography drew Dupigny-Giroux to the field of climatology. "I was always interested in a bird's-eye view of the world around us and trying to figure out the patterns that I observed,"[25] she recalls.

The ability to analyze information and solve problems are important skills for environmental scientists. They need to understand how to investigate a problem, analyze the data they gather, and use the results to determine the best way to address the issue. They may work alone, which requires self-discipline to get their work done.

Collaboration and communication skills are also important because environmental scientists may work with other scientists, as well as engineers and technicians, to study environmental

Getting the Word Out

"Communication is arguably the most important aspect of being an environmental scientist. What I find most rewarding is talking to nonscientists about environmental science, especially kids. I love watching kids' eyes light up when I explain to them what I do because it gives me hope that I've inspired someone."

—Madison Trowbridge, environmental scientist

Quoted in Southwest Florida Water Management District, "A Day in the Life of an Environmental Scientist," *WaterMatters Blog*, April 13, 2021. www.swfwmd.state.fl.us.

issues. At the University of California, Riverside, environmental scientists are working with chemical engineers to get rid of "forever chemicals." These pollutants can contaminate water, soil, fish, livestock, and humans. They break down slowly and can build up in the body, increasing the risk for cancer and other health concerns. The process the scientists are developing looks to destroy the dangerous chemicals by using a combination of hydrogen and light. "After the interaction, hydrogen will become water," explains Haizhou Liu, an associate professor of chemical and environmental engineering. "The advantage of this technology is that it is very sustainable."[26]

Working Conditions

Environmental scientists may work outdoors in the field in all types of weather to gather data and make observations. They might be on a boat to put a sensor on a buoy or travel to the Arctic to drill holes in the ice and gather samples.

They also work in an office or lab setting to analyze findings and read about research done by others. When presenting information, they may be in a classroom, at a conference, or in a business meeting.

Research results may be published or presented at a conference. Some environmental scientists work at universities, and others present information to grade school, middle school, and high school students and the general public. Their research results or information about pollution control is shared in a way that is easier for nonscientists to understand.

Employers and Earnings

Almost half of environmental scientists work for government agencies. They may help reduce air pollution, ensure that water is safe to drink, or develop regulations.

Environmental scientists may also work for scientific or technical consulting companies that help businesses comply with regulations in order to make as little impact on the environment as possible. They may also work with an engineering services firm.

The median pay for an environmental scientist is $76,530, according to the Bureau of Labor Statistics. The highest salary is earned by environmental scientists working for the federal government, who make $103,530 a year. Those working for engineering services firms make $77,450 annually.

Future Outlook

The job outlook for environmental scientists is good because they will be needed to analyze hazards, find solutions to environmental problems, prevent pollution, and help keep communities healthy. Employment is expected to grow by 5 percent through 2031, which is about as fast as job growth for all occupations. The Bureau of Labor Statistics expects about seventy-eight hundred job openings for environmental scientists and specialists each year.

Find Out More

Ecological Society of America
www.esa.org
This professional organization for environmental scientists helps them stay on top of trends and changes in the field. The site's

"Next Generation Careers" page offers a look at internship opportunities. The publications on the website provide a look at the latest research in ecology and the environment.

EnvironmentalScience.org
www.environmentalscience.org
This website, sponsored by university environmental educational programs, explains environmental science and looks at career options. Information is presented about environmental science degrees in each state as well as scholarship opportunities.

University Corporation for Atmospheric Research Center for Science Education
http://scied.ucar.edu
This website encourages students to explore science and gives them a look at STEM careers. It includes profiles of atmospheric science professionals and videos showing interviews with experts from the National Center for Atmospheric Research and University Corporation for Atmospheric Research. The website also has information about internship opportunities.

Biomedical Engineer

What Does a Biomedical Engineer Do?

Helping people with heart disease is the goal of biomedical engineers Luyao Lu and Igor Efimov. They are working on a small, flexible device—about the size of a postage stamp—that monitors heartbeats and helps restore normal rhythm if the heart starts beating erratically. The device contains a grid of microscopic electrodes and can be placed on different areas of the heart to show which are working well. The tiny, soft device is transparent, so doctors can still see the heart when doing a procedure. Another unique feature is that the device is designed to be temporary: it dissolves after six weeks. "Many patients need a temporary device to diagnose their medical condition and provide therapy,"[27] Efimov notes.

Eric Nauman also has a goal of helping people support good health. He wants to keep football players from getting concussions. To do this, the biomedical engineer from the University of Cincinnati looked at how helmets cut down on the impact of hits to the head. For his research, he tested helmets made by several manufacturers. "None of the helmets was uniformly good or

A Few Facts

Number of Jobs
17,900

Pay
$97,410 per year

Educational Requirements
Bachelor's degree in biomedical engineering or related engineering field

Personal Qualities
Analytical, communication, problem-solving skills, creativity

Work Settings
Research lab, health care facility, factory

Future Job Outlook
Projected to grow by 10 percent through 2031

uniformly bad, except on the back of the helmet where they were all uniformly bad," he says. "If you can design a helmet to protect players from the smaller, more typical hits, that would be ideal."[28]

Product design also played a role in the work done by biomedical engineering students at Tulane University in New Orleans, Louisiana. They aimed to improve the lives of young children who need to use wheelchairs. The students and their instructors made small training wheelchairs that help young children with cerebral palsy, spina bifida, or limb deficiencies learn to use a standard wheelchair. The group partnered with a nonprofit organization to design and produce the training wheelchairs. "The design was fairly new, so we had to work through a couple of issues with the assembly, but we were able to work together, and the chairs looked great in the end,"[29] states Anna LeJeune, a biomedical engineering major who was part of the project team.

Biomedical engineers create medical devices that improve people's lives. They use their knowledge of science and engineering to create equipment that prevents injuries, helps doctors treat patients, and enriches the way people live. They might develop artificial organs, make body-part replacements, or come up with a new tool that helps medical professionals make a diagnosis. Biomedical engineers also create software systems and conduct research that advances understanding in the medical field.

The Workday

As an analyst working with robotics and intelligent automation, bioengineering graduate Ornaith O'Reilly splits her time between managing projects for clients and working on software development. "Typically, I spend half my day working 'behind the scenes' building and managing automation solutions," she explains. The rest of her day is spent managing a project for a client, which involves creating and delivering presentations to senior team members and clients and reporting on the project's progress. "While the two projects appear very different, I really like the variety they give me and how they allow me to grow both technical and soft skills,"[30] she says.

Life as a Graduate Student

"My days can be a little busy. A lot of my classes are project based, so I spend most of my time working on projects instead of studying for tests. I like this a lot better because I get to apply my knowledge to real life applications. I also am running a few pilot studies with about eight different nursing homes in the area to test our contamination sanitization inspection and disinfection device.... This is very important and exciting for me because I have a background in long-term care, and this impacts those with compromised immune systems who live in these facilities."

—Kaylee, a biomedical engineering graduate student at the University of North Dakota

Quoted in Allison Osmanson, "Biomedical Engineering Student Spotlight," *All Together* (blog), Society of Women Engineers, November 29, 2021. https://alltogether.swe.org.

Biomedical engineer Saloni Verma develops miniature devices that automatically re-create lab processes, an area of biomedical engineering called microfluidics or lab-on-chip technology. "Think of every single huge lab process, if we could make a chip out of them. What's the best way to automate these technologies?" she asks. "That's what I work with." Her day involves spending time in the lab, working with fluid samples, and analyzing data on a computer. "We do months and months of feasibility testing to introduce a product into the market,"[31] she explains. She also meets with her peers to discuss projects and does training sessions on products at hospitals.

A day for María Álvarez Caballero, a biomedical engineer and quality manager, involves working with 3-D printing technology that creates medical equipment. Her daily tasks include working with product design, development, and documentation as well as monitoring the quality management system to ensure products are properly produced and safe for patients.

Education and Training

A bachelor's degree in biomedical engineering is required for those working in the field. To prepare to study biomedical engineering in college, high school students should emphasize math and science classes. This includes chemistry, physics, and biology, as well as algebra, geometry, trigonometry, and calculus. Computer programming, drafting, and mechanical drawing classes are also useful.

A biomedical bachelor's degree program often includes classes in engineering design, calculus, physics, biology, chemistry, and biomedical engineering. Academic writing and computer programming courses are also part of the curriculum. Biomedical engineers can specialize in an area such as medical images or instruments, biomaterials, or tissue engineering.

Students often gain experience in the field through internships with a hospital, lab, or medical device manufacturer. They may also work with clients as part of a class. "Designers need to understand the needs deeply in order to solve them," stresses Katherine Raymond, a biomedical engineering professor at Tulane University. "[Biomedical engineering] students do a great deal of researching, shadowing and interviewing before they even begin to ideate their solutions for medical problems."[32]

Skills and Personality

Attention to detail is critical because biomedical engineers make products and processes that impact medical decisions. The new devices Verma works with undergo extensive quality control testing at all steps of the product creation process, from design to manufacturing. "At the end of the day we're dealing with biology-based products and it's people's lives that these things are testing,"[33] she notes.

Biomedical engineers must have the math skills necessary to design and analyze products, but they also need to be creative to develop new products and come up with innovative solutions. Álvarez Caballero points to "curiosity, willingness to learn, con-

Biomedical engineers develop medical devices and equipment that improve people's lives. They might develop artificial organs, new diagnostic tools, or, as seen here, a robotic arm.

tinuous improvement of . . . one's own skills and . . . being open to constant challenges"[34] as keys to making a biomedical engineer a valuable member of a team.

Communication skills are also important because biomedical engineers share information and engage in discussions with patients, therapists, clients, other scientists, and medical professionals. They need to be able to analyze the information they gather and have a solid understanding of what is needed by patients and clients. Writing reports and research papers can also be part of their job. Biomedical engineers often work as part of a team, but they also need to work on their own to solve challenging problems.

Working Conditions

Biomedical engineers work in labs, offices, manufacturing facilities, and health care settings. Their work location on any given day will depend on which part of a project they are working on. They are often part of a team, working with scientists, health care workers, and other engineers.

Do Not Keep Ideas to Yourself

"Science is a people business. Bioengineering is primarily about communication and brainstorming exciting ideas with others, the opportunity to bring fresh ideas and fresh faces to the table when solving problems."

—Manu Platt, director of the Biomedical Engineering and Technology Acceleration Center at the National Institutes of Health

Quoted in Stephen Andrews, "Bioengineering to Advance by Collaboration and Inclusion," *NIH Catalyst*, July–August 2023. https://irp.nih.gov.

When conducting research, biomedical engineers spend time in a lab. A meeting with a project team takes place in an office. They also work in a health care setting to train individuals on the use of a device and make sure it is working properly. They may also work in a manufacturing facility to oversee the quality of the devices being made and work on any necessary adjustments to the process.

Employers and Earnings

Biomedical engineers work for medical equipment manufacturing companies, medical supply firms, and health care companies. They also conduct research and development for corporations and at colleges and universities.

In 2021, the median pay for biomedical engineers (where half earn more than that amount and half earn less) was $97,410, according to the Bureau of Labor Statistics. This is more than double the median wage for all occupations in the United States.

The highest earners made more than $154,000 a year, according to the Bureau of Labor Statistics. The highest-paying industry for biomedical engineers is the electromedical, measuring, and control instruments manufacturing industry. Those working in this industry had the highest median wage: $108,690. Working in research and development for the physical, engineering, and life sciences industry brought the second-highest median wage of $98,610, just above the $97,090 median wage for those working in the medical equipment and supplies manufacturing industry. The median wage for those working in health care was $79,400, and people working for colleges and universities earned a median wage of $62,650.

Future Outlook

The number of job openings for biomedical engineers is expected to increase significantly by 2031. The Bureau of Labor Statistics projects employment to grow by 10 percent, which is twice the growth rate projected for all occupations. The bureau expects an additional 1,700 people to be working as bioengineers and biomedical engineers, bringing projected employment in the field to 19,700.

The growing need for medical devices such as prosthetic limbs, surgical tools, and imaging systems brings many career possibilities to bioengineers. As people become more aware of how medical advances can improve their lives, biomedical engineers will be needed to develop new products and services that solve complex medical problems and allow people to overcome injuries and physical limitations. The demand for ways to make it easier and less expensive to quickly diagnose and treat diseases continues to grow, and biomedical engineers will be called upon to create and test new techniques.

Find Out More

American Society of Mechanical Engineers: Content
www.asme.org/topics-resources/content
The latest trends in mechanical engineering are featured on the content website of the American Society of Mechanical Engineers. The website includes podcasts and articles on innovations. There are also quizzes that allow people to test their knowledge of scientific inventions.

Biomedical Engineering Society

www.bmes.org/faqs-about-bme

This FAQ website from the Biomedical Engineering Society offers an overview of focus areas in which biomedical engineering students can specialize and provides examples of biomedical engineering projects. The page also includes a link to an accredited programs website where students can search for colleges offering biomedical engineering degrees.

IEEE.tv

https://ieeetv.ieee.org

This website from the Institute of Electrical and Electronics Engineers (IEEE), an organization for individuals with careers in technology, features videos relating to innovations in science and technology. It includes a web page dedicated to videos for student members. The events tab provides information on conferences.

Society of Women Engineers

https://swe.org

This organization supports women engineers with career resources, professional development content, and networking opportunities. It offers courses for students that provide an overview of biomedical engineering and other engineering specialties. Information about scholarships available to students preparing for careers in engineering and related fields is provided.

Materials Scientist

What Does a Materials Scientist Do?

Olivia Graeve's job is to break things. The materials scientist and her team are working to create a durable steel coating and need to see how much force it can withstand. The protective coating will be used on satellites, and to find out how strong it is, they test it to the point of failure. The goal, Graeve says, is to learn how the material will perform in space—in other words, "how much can you impact it with a meteorite before it breaks?"[35]

Materials scientist Dirk Jordan works with clean energy at the National Renewable Energy Laboratory in Golden, Colorado, and looks to ensure that these energy sources are reliable. To that end, he is studying how solar panels are impacted by extreme weather, such as hurricanes, tornadoes, and hail. "We need to know more about how these events impact current technologies,"[36] he explains.

Materials scientists and engineers create materials and test them to learn their properties. They find innovative ways to make materials for products that are used every day, from dental fillings to dinner plates. A smartphone, car

A Few Facts

Number of Jobs
7,000

Pay
$100,090 per year

Educational Requirements
Bachelor's degree in chemistry or a related physical science field; master's degree or doctorate may be needed for research positions

Personal Qualities
Analytical, communication, interpersonal, problem-solving, time management, organization skills, perseverance

Work Settings
Laboratories, offices, factories

Future Job Outlook
Projected growth of 6 percent through 2031

tire, artificial knee, and refrigerator all contain synthetic materials developed and enhanced by materials scientists.

To better understand how to develop materials that behave the way they want them to, materials scientists do a deep dive into the natural and synthetic substances that make up a material. They analyze the properties and chemical structure to learn more about them and combine them in new ways. To do this, they apply knowledge of math, chemistry, biology, and physics.

A Typical Workday

The work a materials scientist does may revolve around a specific type of material, such as glass, ceramics, or metals. Although they may spend their day working on new products, materials scientists could also have a job that focuses on finding out why a product or material failed and broke down. As a failure analysis engineer for an aircraft engine company, Alyssa Denno tries to figure out why a part corroded or fractured. She works with a team to find the root cause of the problem. Her work involves spending time in the lab, where she uses scientific techniques to analyze coating loss or corrosion of gas turbine engine parts. "I have never been able to sit and read a text book for hours, even now I prefer to spend my work day primarily in the lab, working hands-on with hardware," Denno admits. Her work is not solitary, however. "In a typical work day I interact with multiple different engineering and program groups,"[37] she says. Her coworkers have different areas of specialization, such as structure or design engineering, and are analyzing how those aspects could have contributed to the problem. Denno and the other team members share their findings as they all work to find the root cause of a problem and determine how to correct it.

Materials scientists often work with a team that may include engineers, physicists, and microbiologists. Each member of the team has knowledge in a specific area, and it is the job of a materials scientist to understand the properties of a certain substance and how this impacts the problem the team is looking to solve.

Enjoying Innovation on a Daily Basis

"My favorite part about being a materials engineer is that new discoveries are happening every day in our field. We find material failure conditions that kick off multi-year investigations and lead to metallurgical discoveries, innovations, and even patents. Every single day I work I learn something new!"

—Alyssa Denno, who has a degree in materials science engineering and works as a failure analysis engineer for an aircraft engine company

Quoted in Emily Tacopina, "A Day in the Life of a Material and Science Engineer: Alyssa Denno," *All Together* (blog), Society of Women Engineers, February 3, 2023. https://alltogether.swe.org.

To do their analysis and understand how chemicals interact with each other, they use computers and lab equipment. To analyze the structure of complex molecules, they may use software that creates a 3-D model.

Qian Li, a materials science doctoral student researching bone tissue engineering, works in a university lab with other students. Wearing lab coats, goggles, and gloves, Li conducts experiments on large molecules called polymers, analyzing and testing results using computer programs. In addition, Li researches how these findings can be applied to the ultimate goal of supporting bone tissue regeneration.

Education and Training

A bachelor's degree in chemistry or materials science, or a related scientific field such as physics, is needed to become a materials scientist. Some college engineering programs give students the opportunity to get a degree in materials science and engineering. A materials scientist may specialize in a certain area, such as ceramics, polymers, metals, or semiconductors.

Materials scientists create and test the materials used in the manufacturing of items ranging from dental fillings and dinner plates to refrigerators and solar panels. Those who work with solar panels might study how they will fare in extreme weather.

An eye-opening course for Denno was in failure analysis. "That course taught me that failure is inevitable, in every aspect of life, not just engineering," she explains. "Perfection doesn't exist. But the greatest opportunities to learn and grow and map out a new path to success is through failure. People tend to shy away from and paint it in a negative light and yes there are sometimes very painful losses that come with failure but they are entirely enriched in the opportunity to make something smarter, safer, stronger."[38]

A materials scientist conducting research often needs to acquire more education and earn a master's or doctorate degree. Denno majored in materials science engineering and earned her master's degree in materials process engineering. Jordan, in contrast, has a doctorate in physics and advises students to be familiar with statistics. "There are technical experts, and statisticians, but people with both skillsets are needed,"[39] he says.

Materials scientists need lab experience, and they may acquire it through internships, fellowships, or cooperative programs where they spend time working while in school. While in college, Denno became comfortable working with high-tech lab equipment such as X-ray fluorescence instruments, which use X-ray beams to analyze materials. "I found it very empowering to be able to work with such complex equipment and have confidence in the data output,"[40] she comments.

After graduation, Denno gained experience in a variety of areas as a rotational engineer on a company's quality team. This involved short-term work assignments with several different teams. "Being a rotational engineer during my initial years in the industry gave me the broad scope experience to figure out what I really wanted to do within the aerospace industry without committing years at a time to roles that weren't the best fit for me as an individual contributor," she says. "Working in that group was intense and fast paced and really ignited a passion for the investigative aspect of engineering and the industry."[41]

Skills and Personality

Materials scientists need to understand the properties and structure of materials, so knowledge of physics, chemistry, and engineering are important. Math skills in calculus, algebra, and statistics are needed when conducting research and analysis and to ensure that findings are accurate.

In addition to having technical skills, materials scientists need to be well organized so they can properly conduct experiments and document the results. Their work will likely have deadlines, so they need to manage their time and prioritize tasks to complete a project on time.

The findings of materials scientists need to be shared with others, so good communication skills are required. They may need to deliver presentations and write reports that can be understood by people in their field as well as those without technical knowledge. Because they often work on a team of scientists, engineers, and others, they need strong interpersonal skills. When an experiment does not work as expected, they need to persevere and have the internal motivation to keep trying.

The ability to solve problems is also an asset. Denno notes that this ability has been central to her work—and to her satisfaction with her work. "Problem solving has always been a very rewarding process for me," she notes. "I enjoyed the problem solving aspect of mathematical equations, being faced with a seemingly unsolvable equation at face value but breaking it down into smaller, solvable steps that can be worked through one at a time to reach a solution."[42]

Working Conditions

Materials scientists often work in a laboratory or office. They may need to work late into the day or on the weekend to conduct experiments that need to be done according to a specific time schedule.

While working in the lab, they must follow safety procedures and wear personal protective equipment when handling chemicals. Protective equipment could include goggles, masks, and gloves.

A materials scientist may also visit manufacturing sites. Paula McDonald, who has a degree in materials science and engineering, worked for a company making rocket engines. One of her favorite parts of her job involved traveling in the United States and Europe. "I loved seeing how things were made," she says. "It felt like a field trip."[43]

Employers and Earnings

Materials scientists typically work for government agencies, universities, or companies that make products. They have a median annual wage of $100,090, according to the Bureau of Labor Statistics. Half of all materials scientists earn more than this, and half earn less. The highest-paid materials scientists earn more than $162,950 annually.

The highest-paying employers of materials scientists are in the computer and manufacturing industry. Materials scientists work-

Developing an Interest in Materials Science

"I chose to study Materials Science and Engineering at the University of California, Davis because I had attended an engineering summer residency program in high school. In that program, we tried a different field of engineering every day through different labs, and I discovered Materials Science and Engineering. I loved chemistry and initially wanted to study Chemical Engineering, but I preferred the 'high tech arts and crafts' aspect of Materials Science and Engineering instead. While my first two years of college were challenging, I knew I did not want to change my major. I kept going, continuously improving, and graduated."

—Paula McDonald, materials engineer

Paula McDonald, "Day in the Life of a Materials Engineer," *All Together* (blog), Society of Women Engineers," March 11, 2020. https://alltogether.swe.org.

---

ing in this industry earn a median annual wage of $130,050, the Bureau of Labor Statistics reports. Most materials scientists do scientific research and development, which has a median annual salary of $101,180. Materials scientists may also work in computer and electronic product manufacturing, chemical manufacturing, or services related to engineering.

Future Outlook

The job outlook for materials scientists is promising. Better-quality materials are needed in a variety of areas, from electronics to energy and transportation, and they need to be made economically and safely. Materials scientists will be needed to develop them. The Bureau of Labor Statistics expects 6 percent growth in this field through 2031. This is above the 5 percent job growth rate for all occupations.

Find Out More

American Chemical Society (ACS)

www.acs.org

The society promotes science education and has a web page for students and educators. The high school student site offers information about the Chemistry Olympiad and the ACS Chem-Club. The online *ChemMatters Magazine* features articles on new discoveries and explains scientific concepts.

ASM International: The Materials Information Society

www.asminternational.org

The "Industry News" section on the ASM International website offers information about materials science discoveries from around the world. The society offers networking opportunities for professional members and courses that allow professionals to continue their education.

Materials Today

www.materialstoday.com

This website aims to connect individuals in the materials community. It features news on scientific innovation and discoveries. Podcasts on scientific research are also presented.

Data Scientist

What Does a Data Scientist Do?

As a data scientist, Natalie Morse is a problem solver. "I get to work on new and challenging problems constantly," she says. "I kind of feel like a consultant within the organization. It's really fun to put my thinking hat on and solve problems for different groups."[44]

Data scientists turn massive amounts of data into information that businesses and other entities use to make decisions. They create algorithms and use machine learning, statistics, and natural language processing to mine raw data, clean it up, and present it in a usable format. The data can be used to guide self-driving cars, make manufacturing more efficient, and predict what customers will want to buy. The patterns data scientists uncover help businesses decide where to invest and guide them as they create marketing, sales, and product strategies.

As the head of data science and analytics at a large global energy company, Justin Lo and his team use machine learning to offer insights into what is below the earth's surface. This helps the company improve production and decide where to drill wells. The team is also using AI to determine the best

A Few Facts

Number of Jobs
113,300

Pay
$100,910

Educational Requirements
Bachelor's degree

Personal Qualities
Analytical, communication, problem-solving, logical-thinking skills

Work Settings
Office

Future Job Outlook
Projected to grow 36 percent through 2031

Soaking Up Information

"When we look for entry-level data scientists, more than anything else, we're looking for that curiosity and the ability to be a self-starter. If you're willing to soak up as much information as you can over your first few months, work consistently on your coding skills, and then dive into complicated, interdisciplinary problems, you might be a good fit for a data science team."

—Nick Resnick, lead data scientist

Nick Resnick, "Data Scientist: A Day in the Life," Enterprisers Project, September 15, 2022. https://enterprisersproject.com.

places to store carbon deep underground. The projects that his team works on will help the company protect wildlife while creating less carbon.

Data scientist Nick Resnick leads a team that creates predictive models. Their machine learning pipelines turn data into information that businesses use to improve their operations. The models show patterns and predict what will happen in the future. "Building machine learning pipelines is a large undertaking," Resnick comments. "I've worked on projects that took anywhere from two months to two years from beginning to end."[45]

A Typical Workday

Although each workday is different, Resnick notes that the projects follow a similar path. The team begins by building a predictive model for a customer and gathering the necessary data. "At this stage, we also do a lot of brainstorming, literature review, and algorithm prototyping,"[46] he says.

The next step is to take the prototype and turn it into a model that can be used by a wider audience. The machine learning pipeline is then released as a software update. This requires the team to do a great deal of testing and documentation. Team members also meet with sales and marketing to let them know what the new program can do.

To keep a long-term project on track, Resnick's team sets deadlines for various steps. "If we have a two-month goal, we'll split that into eight two-week sprints, each with its milestones," he explains. "We then use tickets to break apart those milestones into specific code contributions."[47]

Data scientists may also use other project management techniques that help teams collaborate and keep large projects moving forward. They might have a daily meeting where they go over what team members are working on and bring up problems being encountered. They may also use project tracking software that shows how different aspects of a project are progressing. Other techniques include pair programming, where two teammates code alongside each other; one person writes code, and the other checks it for accuracy.

To make sure she is staying on top of her projects, Google data scientist Sundas Khalid checks her calendar and to-do list right after arriving at work. "That helps me set the tone for the day and also gives me an idea of what my day looks like,"[48] she says. Her day typically includes a meeting with her manager and review of a project she is working on. She also documents information about the project and may have a team meeting.

Education and Training

Data scientists use knowledge of computer science, statistics, and analytics. A bachelor's degree in data science, math, statistics, computer science, engineering, or a related field is needed to become a data scientist. A master's degree or doctorate may be required by some employers.

Required classes typically include calculus, linear algebra, statistics, and probability, as well as computer science courses. High school math classes in these areas can help students prepare for their college courses. The information gathered and presented by data scientists has the power to influence people's decisions and behavior, so an ethics course may also be part of their education program.

A data scientist may shift into the role from other science and technology careers. Morse was a graduate student in environmental engineering when she switched her focus. To help get her foot in the door in the tech industry, she got an internship at a tech start-up and took a seven-week boot camp for data scientists after graduation.

Skills and Personality

Data scientists need technical skills in math, statistical modeling, and computer coding. They must understand how to use data visualization tools that allow information to be presented in a way that is relevant and usable. Logical thinking is also required, and data scientists use problem-solving skills to overcome issues and setbacks that can occur when collecting and cleaning data and creating models and algorithms. It also helps to be curious and have a desire to keep learning because the field of data science continually grows and evolves as technology changes.

Communication skills are also important because data scientists share information with people who have varied backgrounds and different levels of technical knowledge. For instance, Resnick's work projects require coordination between data scientists, machine learning engineers, and product managers.

In addition, data scientists need to be aware of any regulations that impact data collection. They also need to be mindful of the implications for the product being created. A product based on data can influence behavior and decisions, and data scientists should understand a product's downsides and risks. "A video-game maker years ago may not have anticipated that some people now would consider their product to be addictive for young children," explains Chris Wiggins, a math professor and chief data scientist at the *New York Times*. "Mitigating harms, in this case, may mean design changes that prevent or lessen extended play or other signs of addictive behavior."[49]

Data scientists turn massive amounts of data into information that businesses and other entities use. These scientists create algorithms and use machine learning, statistics, and natural language processing to mine raw data, clean it up, and present it in a usable format.

Working Conditions

Data scientists spend much of their day sitting at a desk, writing computer code, or in meetings with teammates or clients. They also often meet and work with people from other areas of the company who have expertise in different fields and areas of the business. "Combining these different perspectives is where a lot of the magic happens,"[50] Lo notes.

Although data scientists may go to work at an office, the high demand for data scientists means that companies looking to hire them often allow employees to work remotely. They may come into the office a few days a week or work from home full-time. Resnick works remotely and makes an effort to stay connected with his team. "Our team has implemented some rituals to make sure we get to see each other and make each other laugh," he says. "While it's almost blasphemous for an engineer to say this, I enjoy meetings because of the structure and change of pace they bring to the day, so I often schedule colleague check-ins throughout the week."[51]

Finding New Ways to Solve Complicated Problems

"I work with complex problems crossing many different groups and areas of the business. I work mainly in Python and develop machine learning (ML) or Artificial Intelligence (AI) models. This is a unique role, as I am part of the IT Innovations and Research group. We have the benefit of working on cutting-edge problems, and bringing new ideas and technology."

—Natalie Morse, data scientist

Quoted in Careershifters, "From Environmental Engineer to Data Sscientist." www.careershifters.org.

Employers and Earnings

Many different types of organizations rely on data to make decisions. Although data scientists often work for tech and internet companies, many work for companies involved in health care, manufacturing, agriculture, and finance. Others work for insurance carriers or companies that offer consulting services. In addition, some data scientists manage companies or conduct scientific research. "What we do will vary according to whether we're working on healthcare issues, something related to autonomous driving, or perhaps exploring some particular aspect of climate change," notes Jeannette Wing, a professor of computer science at Columbia University and coauthor of a data science textbook. "The application of data science is largely defined by the nature of the problem we're looking to solve or the task we're trying to complete."[52]

Wages for data scientists are well-above average. Data scientists earned a median annual wage of $100,910 in 2021, according to the Bureau of Labor Statistics. This means that half of data scientists earned more, and half earned less. Data scientists with the highest-paying jobs earned more than $167,040. Those working in scientific research and development and computer systems design had the highest median salaries, around $102,700. Data scientists managing companies and working for management, scientific, and technical consulting services were not far behind, however, with a median salary of $101,000. These salaries are more than double the median salary of $45,760 for all occupations, and they also are higher than the median salary of $98,680 for math and science occupations.

Future Outlook

There will be plenty of jobs for data scientists in the future because there are more job openings than there are people qualified to fill them. The Bureau of Labor Statistics expects employment in this area to grow by 36 percent through 2031. This is more than seven times the growth rate of 5 percent for all occupations.

The need for data scientists stems from the desire businesses have to make decisions based on data. "Companies are struggling to hire true data scientists," says Brandon Purcell, vice president at an industry analyst firm. "Data scientists have the alchemy to turn data into insights. . . . There's a lot of thought going into how to hire and retain them."[53]

Find Out More

CodeHS
www.codehs.com
This site offers computer science courses for high school students. The data science course includes information on data collection, cleanup, analysis, and visualization. In the course, students write algorithms and build statistical models.

Data Science for Everyone
www.datascience4everyone.org
Created by the University of Chicago's Center for Radical Innovation for Social Change, this organization's goal is to advance data

science education. The learning center offers resources for building data science skills. The news section has information about camps and conferences.

Towards Data Science
https://towardsdatascience.com
This site offers information on technological innovations. Articles focus on problem-solving, writing code, and developments in computer technology. A membership provides access to additional articles.

Food Scientist

What Does a Food Scientist Do?

Food scientist Qingrong Huang has created a type of chocolate with two advantages: it is healthier and can be fashioned into any shape. "Everybody likes to eat chocolate, but we are also concerned with our health," comments Huang, a Rutgers University professor. "To address this, we have created a chocolate that is not only low-fat, but that can also be printed with a 3D printer. It's our first 'functional' chocolate."[54]

The creation of nutritious plant-based foods is the focus of food scientist David Julian McClements's work. "There's a huge interest in plant-based foods for improved sustainability, health, and ethical reasons," explains McClements, a food design and nanotechnology expert. "We aim to design them to have all the vitamins and minerals you need and have health-promoting components like dietary fiber and phytochemicals so that they taste good and they're convenient and they're cheap and you can easily incorporate them into your life. That's the goal."[55]

Food scientists develop ways to make foods healthier, safer, and more appealing. They use their knowledge

A Few Facts

Number of Jobs
14,400

Pay
$78,340 per year

Educational Requirements
Bachelor's degree in food science; many earn advanced degrees

Personal Qualities
Analytical, communication, critical-thinking, observation skills, attention to detail

Work Settings
Laboratory, office, may travel to field locations

Future Job Outlook
Projected to grow by 8 percent through 2031

of the chemical makeup of food, and its physical properties, to improve food production, packaging, taste, and preservation. They look for ways to reduce food waste, find new food sources, and keep food from becoming contaminated.

Because they understand how ingredients interact with each other, and how they impact the look and texture of a food product, food scientists have, for example, used paprika to color foods and bulk up foods with fiber from beet sugar. They can also make soda taste like root beer or bacon, give cereal a spicy flavor, and keep deli meats from spoiling. "Every single item of food or beverage you buy in a grocery store has been influenced by a food scientist," says Adam Yee, a food scientist who works for a health and wellness company. "We are indeed responsible for adding preservatives to soda but we are also responsible for finding a way NOT to use preservatives, while also lowering the calories."[56]

The Workday

Senior scientist Devin Lewis works in product development for a global beverage company. His workday varies according to a product's stage in the production process. When an idea is introduced by the marketing team, he creates a flavor profile for it. "I basically have to make that idea come to life," he explains. If he is creating an orange-flavored product, for example, he must determine exactly how it should taste. "You can have zesty, you can have peely, you can have a sweet orange," he notes. "It's understanding what tonalities and what flavor profile you'd like."[57] He also must account for how the ingredients interact with each other. One complex project involved combining coffee and cola. "When you add that to the cola matrix there are some very interesting interactions that occur,"[58] he says.

Food scientists develop product formulas and conduct experiments in a lab, also called doing "bench work." They often do taste tests to determine whether a product has the desired qualities. "Food product development is a science as well as an art," comments Asim Syed, a research and development team leader.

Testing to Ensure Quality

"In a normal product development scenario, we do a lot of shelf life testing to ensure that the quality is consistent throughout the entire shelf life of the product. When you turn a can over, or a bottle over, and read the best buy date that really and truly means something. That guarantees that the quality will be consistent until that date."

—Devin Lewis, senior food scientist

Quoted in Inquire Higher, "A Day in the Life of a Food Scientist Featuring Devin Lewis," *Black Student Success Podcast,* YouTube, January 27, 2022. www.youtube.com/watch?v=h5myqeURaJ0.

"You can do the science through graphs and charts, data analyses, and technical reviews, but you cannot excel in art without touching, feeling, smelling and tasting the food."[59]

If problems emerge during a trial period for a new product, or during production, food scientists step in. Lewis had to resolve a foaming issue with a soda he helped create. "It took four to six weeks of troubleshooting to find the root cause of the issue and then develop so the issue would not reoccur throughout the entire shelf life of the product,"[60] he says.

Food products must also meet government standards for safety and quality. For this reason, food scientists may also spend time researching regulations and making sure a product complies with those requirements.

Education and Training

Food scientists need at least a bachelor's degree from a postsecondary institution, and many have master's degrees. They take general chemistry, physics, calculus, and statistics classes in addition to science classes with a food focus. These can include food chemistry, food safety, quality assurance, and food composition

Food scientists develop ways to make foods healthier, safer, and more appealing. They use their knowledge of the physical properties and chemical makeup of food to prevent contamination and improve food production, packaging, and taste.

as well as food engineering, microbiology, and processing. Students may also take classes in food laws, food service operations, and product development.

Food science students also study sensory analysis and taste foods to learn how various ingredients and processes make an impact. "We use sensory analysis a lot in the food industry because people actually have to like the taste of the food being sold,"[61] Yee explains.

Courses may also focus on a specific type of food, such as fermented foods, meats, candy, or chocolate. Classes often include lab research, and students gain additional experience through internships. While in graduate school, a food scientist student often conducts original research in a lab and may also supervise undergraduate students.

Skills and Personality

In addition to having a solid understanding of math and science, food scientists need strong communication skills. They must explain the results and impact of their research to fellow scientists as well as to coworkers and members of the public who do not have a technical background. They may provide information through reports or in-person presentations.

Food scientists also need to be skilled in collecting information, making observations, and analyzing data. To determine the best way to conduct research or solve a problem, they need critical-thinking skills, curiosity, and persistence. "Persistence will definitely take you a long way," Lewis says. "Doors will open, but maybe not on the first knock, maybe not on the second knock. But having that persistence and that conviction to follow through with what you're trying to achieve, that will definitely come in handy." A food scientist also needs to feel comfortable in reaching out to colleagues when help is needed. "You can't just throw in the towel and say this is not going to work," Lewis points out. "You've got stakeholders, you've got shareholders to consider, you've got a timeline that you've got to meet. Saying that this doesn't work is not going to cut it."[62]

Working Conditions

A laboratory is often the setting for a food scientist's work. It is where food scientists conduct experiments and gather data, often according to their own research methods with little supervision. They may lead teams of students or technicians who assist with research. When working in a lab, they wear personal protective equipment such as goggles and gloves.

Food scientists also work at a computer to create reports, conduct research, and analyze results. They may attend conferences to present their findings as well as to learn about trends and developments in the industry.

A food scientist may work on the production floor of a food manufacturing facility. "I spent the first four years of my career on the

Stumbling Upon the Perfect Career

"I began as an undergraduate at Penn State majoring in nutrition science because I wanted to have a scientific degree. . . . I literally stumbled onto food science. I felt like I had found a diamond in the rough, a rare treasure that combined something most people love—food—with my own love of the sciences. Food science was balanced and offered a bit of everything. I studied biology, chemistry, biochemistry, microbiology, physics, statistics, experimental design, and product development. . . . It was the first time I felt passionate about an area of study. I felt like I had found my tribe."

—Julie Emsing Mann, food scientist

Julie Emsing Mann, "Embracing the Accidental Food Scientist," Institute of Food Technologists, May 30, 2023. www.ift.org.

---

production floor, managing production lines and leading production staff and operations," states Syed. "Those four years . . . helped me immensely in being able to relate the bench top development work with the limitations and complexities of the production line."[63]

To oversee production of a new product, a food scientist may need to travel to a manufacturing site. "Sometimes these trips can last one day, or a month," Yee says. "It depends on how vital it is, but just the thought of failing a successful launch will give you plenty of reasons to live in a hotel for a week."[64]

Employers and Earnings

Food scientists often work for food manufacturing companies, government agencies, or universities. Companies that make food products—from cereal to yogurt to pizza—need food scientists to analyze ingredients, conduct research, and develop new items. "If you can think of your favorite food, your favorite packaged food, the company that puts that out, a food scientist is going to work for that company,"[65] Lewis notes. Food scientists also conduct research for government agencies to ensure food products meet regulatory standards. They also may conduct research and teach at universities or work for scientific or technical consulting services.

The Bureau of Labor Statistics reports that food scientists earn more than the average worker. The median wage for food scientists is $78,340 a year. Half of all food scientists earn more than this amount, and half earn less. This is much higher than the median wage for all occupations of $45,760. The highest-paid food scientists work in research and development and earn a median annual wage of $86,330. Those working in food manufacturing earn $77,490 per year, and those working for a government agency earn a median annual wage of $73,490.

Future Outlook

The number of jobs in food science is expected to grow by 8 percent by 2031, faster than the average growth of 5 percent for all occupations. The need for better food processing techniques and the demand for tastier, healthier, more nutritious food drives the need for food scientists. Trends can lead to a demand for food scientists with knowledge in a specific area, as McClements found with the movement toward plant-based foods. "There's a huge amount of innovation and investment in this area, and I get contacted frequently by different startup companies who are trying to make plant-based fish or eggs or cheese, but who often don't have a background in the science of foods,"[66] he explains.

Find Out More

FoodGrads
www.foodgrads.com
This website connects students, graduates, and employers in the food and beverage industry. The "Students and Grads" section offers information about career paths, and it includes a podcast section where professionals working in the food and beverage industry share information about their jobs.

Institute of Food Technologists

www.ift.org

The organization has provided collaboration opportunities for food professionals since 1939. Its website offers food science news and has a section for students; student memberships also are available.

ScienceDaily

www.sciencedaily.com

This website is a resource for all types of science news, including information about food science. It offers articles on breaking news and trending topics.

Source Notes

Introduction: Jobs That Can Change the World

1. Quoted in *U.S. News & World Report,* "Biomedical Engineer Overview." https://money.usnews.com.
2. Quoted in Ames National Laboratory, "Structure of the Elusive Boron Monoxide Finally Determined After 83 Years," Newswise, July 18, 2023. www.newswise.com.
3. Quoted in Career Girls, "Artificial Intelligence CEO: How to Develop Self-Confidence—Marilyn Jackson Career Girls." www.careergirls.org.
4. Quoted in Career Girls, "Artificial Intelligence CEO."
5. Quoted in Career Girls, "Artificial Intelligence CEO."

AI Computer and Information Research Scientist

6. Quoted in Kyle Wiggers, "Gantry Launches out of Stealth to Help Data Scientists Keep AI Models Fresh," TechCrunch, June 7, 2022. https://techcrunch.com.
7. Quoted in Association for Computing Machinery, "People of ACM: Jun Kato," April 25, 2023. www.acm.org.
8. Quoted in Wayne State University Division of Research, "Wayne State to Develop Application to Conduct Automated Motivational Interviewing Counseling Focused on Weight Loss," Newswise, June 1, 2023. www.newswise.com.
9. Quoted in Gemma Conroy et al., "Six Researchers Who Are Shaping the Future of Artificial Intelligence," *Nature*, December 2020. www.nature.com.
10. Rik Koncel-Kedziorski, "A Day in the Life of an AI Researcher," *Kensho Blog,* May 16, 2023. https://blog.kensho.com.
11. Koncel-Kedziorski, "A Day in the Life of an AI Researcher."
12. Koncel-Kedziorski, "A Day in the Life of an AI Researcher."
13. Nicolai Nielsen, "A Day in the Life as an AI Engineer," YouTube, January 26, 2023. www.youtube.com/watch?v=n8QxPlceeN8.
14. Quoted in JPMorgan, "Life as an AI Researcher & Machine Learning Engineer," YouTube, February 27, 2020. www.youtube.com/watch?v=kKYIoh7_k5s.

15. Quoted in Career Girls, "Artificial Intelligence CEO."
16. Quoted in Robert Wiblin and Keiran Harris, "Jan Leike on How to Become a Machine Learning Alignment Researcher," *80,000 Hours* (podcast), March 16, 2018. https://80000hours.org.
17. Quoted in Robert Wiblin and Keiran Harris, "Jan Leike on OpenAI's Massive Push to Make Superintelligence Safe in 4 Years or Less," *80,000 Hours* (podcast), August 7, 2023. https://80000hours.org.

Environmental Scientist

18. Quoted in Southwest Florida Water Management District, "A Day in the Life of an Environmental Scientist," *WaterMatters Blog*, April 13, 2021. www.swfwmd.state.fl.us.
19. Quoted in Lake Champlain Basin Program, "Meet the Scientist: Observations and Patterns with Lesley-Ann Dupigny-Giroux, PhD," YouTube, April 11, 2023. www.youtube.com/watch?v=3SHoomcR_3E.
20. Quoted in American Association for the Advancement of Science, "How Will a Warming World Impact the Earth's Ability to Offset Our Carbon Emissions?," EurekAlert!, June 15, 2023. www.eurekalert.org.
21. Quoted in WGI, "A Day in the Life of an Environmental Scientist: Amanda Montgomery, PWS," June 1, 2021. https://wginc.com.
22. Quoted in Southwest Florida Water Management District, "A Day in the Life of an Environmental Scientist."
23. Quoted in Patricia Tate, "You're a What? Climatologist—Lesley-Ann Dupigny-Giroux," Bureau of Labor Statistics, April 2022. www.bls.gov.
24. Quoted in Lake Champlain Basin Program, "Meet the Scientist."
25. Quoted in Tate, "You're a What?"
26. Quoted in David Danelski, "Pollution Cleanup Method Destroys Toxic 'Forever Chemicals,'" UC Riverside News, December 12, 2022. https://news.ucr.edu.

Biomedical Engineer

27. Quoted in Charles Choi, "Flexible Implant Treats Heart Disease, Then Dissolves," *IEEE Spectrum,* July 14, 2023. https://spectrum.ieee.org.
28. Quoted in Michael Miller, "NYT: Collective Force Increases Odds of Football Concussions," UC News, June 20, 2023. www.uc.edu.
29. Quoted in Barri Bronston, "Biomedical Engineering Students Team Up to Design and Make Child-Size Wheelchairs," Tulane News, June 22, 2023. https://news.tulane.edu.
30. Quoted in Silicon Republic, "Meet the Bioengineering Graduate Now Working as a Tech Consultant," September 22, 2022. www.siliconrepublic.com.

31. Saloni Verma, "Day in the Life of a Biomedical Engineer," YouTube, January 25, 2021. www.youtube.com/watch?v=yA5Oo4aGczo.
32. Quoted in Bronston, "Biomedical Engineering Students Team Up to Design and Make Child-Size Wheelchairs."
33. Verma, "Day in the Life of a Biomedical Engineer."
34. Quoted in Madeleine P., "#Working 3D: Six Questions for a 3D Printing Biomedical Engineer," 3D Natives, July 11, 2023. www.3dnatives.com.

Materials Scientist

35. Quoted in Mission Unstoppable, "What Does a Materials Scientist Do?," YouTube, August 19, 2021. www.youtube.com/watch?v=9at6Tm4e-qY.
36. Quoted in Ernie Tucker, "Distinguished Researcher Dirk Jordan Knows the Value of Long-Term Reliability," National Renewable Energy Laboratory, July 28, 2023. www.nrel.gov.
37. Quoted in Emily Tacopina, "A Day in the Life of a Material and Science Engineer: Alyssa Denno," *All Together* (blog), Society of Women Engineers, February 3, 2023. https://alltogether.swe.org.
38. Quoted in Tacopina, "A Day in the Life of a Material and Science Engineer."
39. Quoted in Tucker, "Distinguished Researcher Dirk Jordan Knows the Value of Long-Term Reliability."
40. Quoted in Tacopina, "A Day in the Life of a Material and Science Engineer."
41. Quoted in Tacopina, "A Day in the Life of a Material and Science Engineer."
42. Quoted in Tacopina, "A Day in the Life of a Material and Science Engineer."
43. Paula McDonald, "Day in the Life of a Materials Engineer," *All Together* (blog), Society of Women Engineers, March 11, 2020. https://alltogether.swe.org.

Data Scientist

44. Quoted in Careershifters, "From Environmental Engineer to Data Scientist." www.careershifters.org.
45. Nick Resnick, "Data Scientist: A Day in the Life," Enterprisers Project, September 15, 2022. https://enterprisersproject.com.
46. Resnick, "Data Scientist."
47. Resnick, "Data Scientist."
48. Sundas Khalid, "A Day in the Life of a Google Data Scientist (Analytics)," YouTube, October 7, 2021. https://www.youtube.com/watch?v=CSdpk6NzvhY.

49. Quoted in Association for Computing Machinery, "More than Just Algorithms: A Discussion with Alfred Spector, Peter Norvig, Chris Wiggins, Jeannette Wing, Ben Fried, and Michael Tingley," *ACM Queue,* March 27, 2023. https://queue.acm.org.
50. Quoted in Beena Ammanath, "Chevron Head of Data Science, 'The Industry Has a Big Opportunity,'" *CIO Journal,* May 5, 2023. https://deloitte.wsj.com.
51. Resnick, "Data Scientist."
52. Quoted Association for Computing Machinery, "More than Just Algorithms."
53. Quoted in Sharon Gaudin, "Expert Tips for Hiring (and Retaining) Data Scientists," CIO, September 1, 2022. www.cio.com.

Food Scientist

54. Quoted in Rutgers University, "Want Healthy Valentine Chocolates? We Can Print Them," ScienceDaily, February 14, 2023. www.sciencedaily.com.
55. Quoted in University of Massachusetts–Amherst, "Food Scientists Aim to Make Plant-Based Protein Tastier and Healthier," ScienceDaily, June 4, 2021. www.sciencedaily.com.
56. Adam Yee, "What Is Food Science? A Beginner's Guide," My Food Job Rocks. https://myfoodjobrocks.com.
57. Quoted in Inquire Higher, "A Day in the Life of a Food Scientist Featuring Devin Lewis," *Black Student Success Podcast,* YouTube, January 27, 2022. www.youtube.com/watch?v=h5myqeURaJ0.
58. Quoted in Inquire Higher, "A Day in the Life of a Food Scientist Featuring Devin Lewis."
59. Asim Syed, "A Day in the Life of a Food Scientist," FoodGrads, December 1, 2020. https://foodgrads.com.
60. Quoted in Inquire Higher, "A Day in the Life of a Food Scientist Featuring Devin Lewis."
61. Yee, "What Is Food Science?"
62. Quoted in Inquire Higher, "A Day in the Life of a Food Scientist Featuring Devin Lewis."
63. Syed, "A Day in the Life of a Food Scientist."
64. Adam Yee, "Why You Shouldn't Be a Food Scientist," My Food Job Rocks. https://myfoodjobrocks.com.
65. Quoted in Inquire Higher, "A Day in the Life of a Food Scientist Featuring Devin Lewis."
66. Quoted in University of Massachusetts–Amherst, "Food Scientists Aim to Make Plant-Based Protein Tastier and Healthier."

Interview with a Food Scientist

Luis Rodriguez-Saona is a professor of food science at Ohio State University. Before coming to the university, he worked for the Food and Drug Administration to identify chemical and biological threats in the food supply. He continues to do research in addition to teaching. He talked about the work of food scientists during a phone interview.

Q. Why did you become a food scientist?
A. I was very interested in preservation, the different ways we can extend the shelf life of foods. In Peru, we come from the Incas, and the Incas were a culture that was very advanced in technology associated with preservation. They are the first ones to use lyophilization [freeze-drying] as a means of preserving food. Basically, what they did is play with altitudes in the Andes Mountains so they could actually freeze the meat and potatoes. That was a really clever way that they used to preserve food. That was something I was very intrigued with.

Q. How does the work of a food scientist compare to other jobs in science?
A. We are an applied science. We take from the basic sciences—chemistry, biology, engineering—and we apply it to food. It has very practical applications. If we are trying to prevent the browning of apples, we can use some different chemicals or processing to prevent an apple from oxidizing. How do you tell if it works? Your apple does not develop this brown pigment. It is very practical.

In addition, it is diverse. We have students who are going to be working on how foods are perceived and the different sensations they are going to provide to us. We have chemistry and we are going to look at these reaction pathways that are going to lead to beneficial changes in foods.

Q. How do you use technology in your work?
A. I work with technology that uses electromagnetic radiation. Basically, we play with different wavelengths. We use either light or heat to generate these different radiations, and then we are looking at how different molecules are going to be absorbing this energy.

We are developing sensors that look for target compounds in different foods, so we can understand the level of protein, fat, and sugar. Then we can look for compounds associated with health benefits. We are trying to give farmers, industry, and consumers information so they can make decisions.

We get the information from these sensors and use pattern recognition that allows us to identify unique bands in that spectrum that are associated with the different components. That is what is powerful about our system; we can use a combination of different bands to identify the type of compounds that are present in a sample. Pattern recognition allows us to use this statistical analysis to develop unique algorithms that are going to be predicting the amount of these different compounds.

Q. How is this information used?
A. In our lab we are researching portable and handheld devices that you can take to the field. Everything is geared toward real-time information so you can make fast decisions about your product. In a lot of industries, you cannot wait two weeks to get the lab report because that's too late.

Q. How do the students get the data they need?
A. Students look at samples, they measure different traits, and develop predictive algorithms that are going to encompass different predictive measurements. When we work with tomatoes, for example, the students are going to be running many different tests

on that one sample. We usually have five hundred or six hundred samples, and we measure all these different components.

We develop a predictive algorithm that will have embedded all these different tests. Students are going to develop these algorithms from scratch. We integrate all that into output that is useful for the companies we work with. In the end, information that would take days to find in the lab, we are able to get that information in about thirty seconds.

Q. Who would enjoy a job in food science?
A. If you like the food industry, you are going to find the right fit. As long as people want to eat, you are going to have job security. We're there every time you go to your grocery store.

There is a lot of science that goes into making ice cream, for example. When consumers don't want sugar in their ice cream, we need to come up with alternatives.

We have students who come to our grad school who are from chemistry, biochemistry, and engineering. The common path is that they love food. They want to work in this field. They want to create new food alternatives; they want to investigate phytochemicals that are present and how they lower the risk for chronic diseases. We also do a lot of work with food safety. There are so many different paths, and what unites all that is food.

Other Jobs in Science

Agricultural engineer
Astronomer
Atmospheric scientist
Biochemist
Biophysicist
Chemical engineer
Civil engineer
Computer information systems manager
Computer network architect
Cost estimator
Electrical engineer
Epidemiologist
Food science technician
Industrial engineer
Information security analyst
Geoscientist
Hydrologist
Mechanical engineer
Medical scientist
Meteorologist
Microbiologist
Nuclear engineers
Operations research analyst
Petroleum engineer
Physicist
Plant scientist

Editor's note: The online *Occupational Outlook Handbook* of the US Department of Labor's Bureau of Labor Statistics is an excellent source of information on jobs in hundreds of career fields, including many of those listed here. The *Occupational Outlook Handbook* may be accessed online at www.bls.gov/ooh.

Index

Note: Boldface page numbers indicate illustrations.

AI (artificial intelligence) computer/information research scientist
  education/training requirements, 6, 9
  employers of, 11
  future job outlook, 6, 11
  information on, 12
  number of jobs, 6
  role of, 6–7
  salary/earnings, 6, 11
  skills/personal qualities, 6, 9–11
  typical workday, 7–9
  working conditions, 11
  work settings, 6
Álvarez Caballero, María, 23, 24–25
American Chemical Society (ACS), 36
American Society of Mechanical Engineers: Content, 27
Ames National Laboratory, 4
ASM International: The Materials Information Society, 36

biomedical engineer, **25**
  education/training requirements, 21, 24
  employers of, 26
  future job outlook, 21, 27
  information on, 27–28
  number of jobs, 21
  role of, 21–22
  salary/earnings, 21, 26–27
  skills/personal qualities, 21, 24–25
  typical workday, 22–23
  working conditions, 25–26
  work settings, 21
Biomedical Engineering Society, 28
Breazeal, Cynthia, 7
Bureau of Labor Statistics (BLS)
  on AI computer and information research scientist, 11–12
  on biomedical engineer, 26–27
  on data scientist, 42–43
  on environmental scientist, 19
  on food scientist, 51
  on materials scientist, 34–35
  on STEM occupations, 4, 60

Career Girls (website), 12
climatologist, 14
CodeHS (website), 43

Data Science for Everyone (website), 43–44
data scientist, **41**
  education/training requirements, 37, 39–40
  employers of, 42–43
  future job outlook, 37, 43
  information on, 43–44
  number of jobs, 37
  role of, 37–38
  salary/earnings, 37, 42–43
  skills/personal qualities, 37, 40
  typical workday, 38–39
  working conditions, 40–41
  work settings, 37
Denno, Alyssa, 30, 31, 32–33, 34
Dupigny-Giroux, Lesley-Ann, 13, 15–16, 17

Ecological Society of America, 19–20
Efimov, Igor, 21
environmental chemist, 14
EnvironmentalScience.org, 20
environmental scientist, **16**
  education/training requirements, 13, 16–17
  employers of, 19
  future job outlook, 13, 19
  information on, 19–20
  number of jobs, 13
  role of, 13–14
  salary/earnings, 13, 19
  skills/personal qualities, 13, 17–18
  typical workday, 15–16
  working conditions, 18–19
  work settings, 13

FoodGrads (website), 51
food scientist, **48**
  education/training requirements, 45, 47–48
  employers of, 50–51
  future job outlook, 45, 51
  information on, 51–52
  interview with, 57–59
  number of jobs, 45
  role of, 45–46
  salary/earnings, 45, 51
  skills/personal qualities, 45, 49
  typical workday, 46–47
  working conditions, 49–50
  work settings, 45
Frontiers in Artificial Intelligence (website), 12

Graeve, Olivia, 29

Huang, Qingrong, 45

IEEE Computer Society (website), 12
IEEE.tv (website), 28
industrial ecologist, 14
Institute of Food Technologists, 52
Iowa State University, 4–5

Jackson, Marilyn, 5, 10
Jordan, Dirk, 29, 32

Kato, Jun, 6
Khalid, Sundas, 39
Koncel-Kedziorski, Rik, 7–8
Kotev, Alexander, 6–7

Lavik, Erin, 4

Leike, Jan, 9, 10–11
Lewis, Devin, 46, 47, 49, 50
Li, Qian, 31
Liu, Haizhou, 18
Lo, Justin, 37, 41
Lu, Luyao, 21

Mangu, Lidia, 9
Mann, Julie Emsing, 50
materials scientist, **32**
  education/training requirements, 29, 31–33
  employers of, 34–35
  future job outlook, 29, 35
  information on, 36
  number of jobs, 29
  role of, 29–30
  salary/earnings, 29, 34–35
  skills/personal qualities, 29, 33–34
  typical workday, 30–31
  working conditions, 34
  work settings, 29
Materials Today (website), 36
McClements, David Julian, 45, 51
McDonald, Paula, 34, 35
Montgomery, Amanda, 15, 17
Morse, Natalie, 37, 40, 42

Nauman, Eric, 21–22
Nielsen, Nicolai, 8–9

Occupational Outlook Handbook (Bureau of Labor Statistics), 60
O'Reilly, Ornaith, 22

Perras, Frederic, 5
Platt, Manu, 26

Raymond, Katherine, 24
Resnick, Nick, 38, 39, 40, 41
Rodriguez-Saona, Luis, 57–59
rotational engineer, 33

science, technology, engineering, and mathematics (STEM) occupations, 4
  other jobs in, 60
ScienceDaily (website), 52
Society of Women Engineers, 28
STEM occupations. *See* science, technology, engineering, and mathematics occupations
Sun, Wu, 13–14
Syed, Asim, 46–47, 49–50

Tobin, Josh, 6
Towards Data Science (website), 44
Trowbridge, Madison, 13, 15, 18

University Corporation for Atmospheric Research Center for Science Education, 20
University of California, Riverside, 18

Verma, Saloni, 23, 24

Wiggins, Chris, 40
Wing, Jeannette, 42

Yee, Adam, 46, 48, 50

Picture Credits

Cover: goodluz/Shutterstock

16: VE.Studio/Shutterstock
25: anon-tae/iStock
32: Laurence Dutton/iStock
41: Gorodenkoff/Shutterstock
48: Blue Titan/Shutterstock

About the Author

Terri Dougherty is the author of more than one hundred books for children and teens. She enjoys writing because she loves exploring new ideas and concepts. She lives with her husband in Appleton, Wisconsin. They have three adult children and enjoy hiking, biking, and other outdoor activities.